The Korean War Veterans Memorial

CORNERSTONES OF FREEDOM™

SECOND SERIES

R. Conrad Stein

Children's Press®
A Division of Scholastic Inc.
New York • Toronto • London • Auckland • Sydney
Mexico City • New Delhi • Hong Kong
Danbury, Connecticut

Photographs © 2002: AP/Wide World Photos: 17 (Frank Kerr/U.S. Marine Corps.), 26 (L.M. Otero), 14, 44 bottom (U.S. Dept. of Defense), 4, 22, 27; Corbis Images: 3, 8 bottom, 10 top, 11, 19, 24 (Bettmann), 23 (Horace Bristol), 25 (Philip James Corwin), 13 (James Cox Pfc.), 12 (Hulton-Deutsch Collection), 20 (F. Kazukaitis), 30 (Charles O'Rear); Hulton Archive/Getty Images: cover background, 10 bottom (CNP), 15, 44 top; Scott Boatright: cover bottom right, 5, 7, 8 top, 9, 29, 31, 33, 34, 35, 37, 38, 39, 40, 41, 45 top left, 45 right; Sovfoto/Eastfoto: 16; The Image Works/Rob Crandall: cover top left, 36, 45.

The author wishes to dedicate this book to the wonderful group of marines he served with in Okinawa in 1956: Weapons Company, 3rd Battalion, 9th Regiment, 3rd Marine Division, F.M.F.; Semper Fi, Brothers!

Library of Congress Cataloging-in-Publication Data
Stein, R. Conrad.
   The Korean War Veterans Memorial / R. Conrad Stein
        p.cm.— (Cornerstones of freedom)
   Includes bibliographical references and index.
   ISBN 0-516-22260-0
   1. Korean War Veterans Memorial (Washington, D.C.)—Juvenile literature. 2. Korean War, 1950-1953—Juvenile literature. [1. Korean War Veterans Memorial (Washington, D.C.) 2. Korean War, 1950-1953. 3. National monuments.] I. Title. II. Series.

DS921.92.U6 S74 2001
951.904'26—dc21

                              00-060216

1 2 3 4 5 6 7 8 9 10 R 11 10 09 08 07 06 05 04 03 02

IN 1945 A SOLDIER FROM the town of Terre Haute, Indiana, came home from World War II. The soldier marched in a victory parade down the town's main street. The mayor and all of Terre Haute's prominent people shook his hand. Eight years later the soldier's younger brother returned from the Korean War. There were no parades and few handshakes. Aside from his family, the younger brother's homecoming went unnoticed by the citizens of Terre Haute.

Many people lost friends and loved ones during the Korean War.

THE FORGOTTEN WAR

The Korean War is called the "Forgotten War." The conflict was largely ignored by the American public while it raged. Even today the war is covered by only a few paragraphs, rather than a chapter, in the history books. But those who fought in Korea will never forget the terror and the misery they suffered there. For the rest of their lives they will have painful memories of friends who were killed in that faraway land. Years after the last shot was fired, one soldier said, "I guess I'm lucky. I'm still alive. But oh what it did to me. Oh, God, what [Korea] did to me."

FORGOTTEN NO MORE

On July 27, 1995—exactly forty-two years after the war ended—thousands of people gathered at the National Mall in Washington, D.C. On that day the Korean War Veterans Memorial was officially dedicated. South Korean President Kim Young Sam joined President Bill Clinton at the ceremony. The crowd came to remember

A gathering of Korean War veterans at the dedication on July 27,

A WAR WITHOUT END

Technically, the Korean War never ended. The fighting stopped with a cease-fire. No official peace treaty concluded the conflict.

the Forgotten War. The day dawned brutally hot and muggy. Most of the Korean War veterans present were white-haired men, now in their sixties or seventies. They stood, sweat running down their faces, while President Bill Clinton gave a speech. The president, who was not quite four years old when the Korean War began, said, "The Korean War veteran endured terrible hardships—deathly cold, weeks and months crammed in foxholes. . . . In a struggle so long and consuming, perhaps it is not surprising that too many lost sight of Korea. . . . [But] you put the free world on the road to victory in the Cold War."

Shortly after the speech a sudden thunderstorm ripped out of the Washington sky and drove most of the onlookers home. The veterans, who fought a war in the often unforgiving Korean climate, remained to get a better look at their memorial. Looming above them were nineteen larger-than-life stainless steel statues of men dressed in combat gear. At the feet of the statues are granite rocks and juniper bushes. These stones and shrubs represent the rugged Korean landscape. The figures carry rifles, and they wear sturdy military raincoats called **ponchos**. Each poncho is sculpted so that it seems to blow as if in a fierce wind. The memorial's soldier statues march in a triangular formation toward an American flag. Their expressions show fear, confusion, and weariness—the haunting looks of men at war.

Behind the marching figures is a long granite wall. **Subtly** engraved on that wall are the almost hazy faces of 2,400 American men and women who served in the

The faces of the statues capture the looks of men at war.

The Wall of Faces at the Korean War Veterans Memorial

The Silver Star

Korean War. In sharp contrast to the marchers the faces on the wall are smiling because they are posing for snapshots taken by a buddy. The granite wall is covered with such pictures. The simple photos, frozen in stone, suggest the comradeship fostered by those who have fought together in a brutal war.

As the Korean War veterans admired the monument they spoke with newspaper reporters who had come to do interviews. "Why am I here?" said Tom Waltonbaugh of Pittsburgh. "Here's thirty-five reasons why." He handed a reporter from the *Chicago Tribune* a sheet of paper. On the paper were handwritten names of thirty-five members of his infantry company, all of whom were killed in Korea. "They were the real heroes," said Waltonbaugh.

Angus Deming was another Korean War veteran present for the ceremonies. Deming, a marine lieutenant who won the Silver Star for bravery, was covering the memorial ceremonies for *Newsweek* magazine. He spoke for all Korean servicemen and servicewomen when he wrote, "This was a long-overdue celebration. The Korean War—our war—was no longer lost somewhere between World War II and Vietnam. It was no longer the 'Forgotten War.'"

The veterans remained gathered around the new monument as it grew dark. Many wore T-shirts and hats bearing the names of their old outfits. Some found friends they hadn't seen in more than forty years. All thought back to the war of their youth, the war that changed their lives.

THE MIGHTY T-34

Early in the war the North Korean army was equipped with Russian-built T-34 tanks. These thirty-ton machines were the same type of tanks that helped the Russians defeat the German army in World War II.

A T-34 tank

U.S. troops of the 1st Cavalry Division cross a stream as they move into front lines in Korea during the Korean War.

A DISTANT THUNDER

June 25, 1950, and the time was 3:30 A.M. at the 38th **parallel** in Korea. It was still dark on Sunday morning when muzzle flashes from a thousand cannons suddenly blazed over the North Korean horizon. Huge 122-mm guns roared with blasts that sounded like rolling thunder. Next came the clanging of metal treads as Russian-built tanks rolled over the hills. The tanks were followed by infantry. In this manner the North Korean Army swept into South Korea. Powerful tank-led columns sent South Korean forces reeling backward.

10

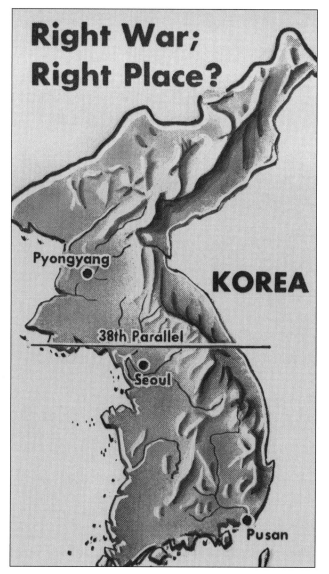

Right War; Right Place?

KOREA

Pyongyang

38th Parallel

Seoul

Pusan

KOREA, A BLOODY HISTORY

Korea is a **peninsula** that sticks out of China like a fat thumb. Early in the twentieth century the entire peninsula was occupied by Japan. During the closing days of World War II (1939–1945) Russian armies drove into northern Korea. The Russians stopped at the 38th parallel, a hastily drawn dividing line across the middle of the peninsula. The line was designed to separate Russian and U.S. occupying armies. At first all parties believed the 38th parallel would only be a temporary boundary. But then a communist government was established in North Korea while a capitalist system developed in South Korea. Korea became a victim of the Cold War, the tense battle of ideologies that gripped the world after World War II.

A map of Korea showing the 38th parallel

Days after the initial invasion American troops stationed in Japan were called to repel the North Korean advance. The sudden call to action caught the Americans entirely by surprise. Most were completely unfamiliar

The UN Security Council meets about the situation in Korea.

with Asian geography. As they boarded ships and air-planes American soldiers were heard to say, "Korea, where the hell is that?"

In the opening stages of the war, American forces and their South Korean allies were pushed down the stem of Korea. Generals called their withdrawal a "fighting retreat." But the men in the field knew they were being beaten by a **relentless** enemy. Finally, the American-led forces dug into a defensive line circling the port city of

Pusan. For six terrible weeks in August and September 1950, the allies held off furious North Korean attacks. Some twenty thousand Americans were killed or wounded defending what was called the Pusan Perimeter.

Ten thousand miles (16,000 kilometers) away, in New York City, delegates to the United Nations (UN) argued about the hostilities in Korea. The UN was founded in 1945 with the goal of promoting world peace. However,

Soldiers in Korean trenches, 1950

★ ★ ★ ★

the Cold War divided countries into Communist and anti-Communist camps, thereby weakening the effectiveness of the world organization. Still, the UN condemned North Korea for its aggression. Twenty-two UN nations promised to send troops to Korea, and eighteen countries actually sent military units. UN members such as Great Britain, France, Turkey, the Netherlands, Austria, and the Philippines were major U.S. partners in the Korean War.

General Douglas MacArthur

U.S. Marines land at Inchon in South Korea.

In Washington, D.C., American political leaders also argued. Most said a war was necessary to defeat Communist aggression. But only a handful of politicians wanted the U.S. Congress to declare war on North Korea. In fact, many influential Americans refused to call the conflict a war at all. Some, including President Truman himself, claimed it was a police action supported by the UN. "Police action" was a hollow term to the men fighting for their lives: This looked like war; it smelled like war; it hurt like war. A grim joke was told along the bloody Pusan Perimeter: "If this is a police action, why don't they send cops?"

On September 15, 1950, three months after the North Korean invasion, American marine and army units landed at Inchon Harbor, far behind enemy lines. It was a daring operation, planned and executed by the World War II hero General Douglas MacArthur. Two weeks later, American forces recaptured Seoul, the capital of South Korea. In early

★ ★ ★ ★

**A soldier in the
Chinese Army**

October, MacArthur's men crossed the 38th parallel and raced into North Korea. By Thanksgiving Day the enemy was judged to be demoralized and beaten, and there was talk of bringing American troops home for Christmas.

But the Korean War then took an ugly turn. From out of the mountains of North Korea more than three hundred thousand Chinese troops streamed down on UN forces. China had become a Communist nation in 1949 and was now a powerful player in the Cold War. The Chinese Army

* * * *

preferred to attack at night. Lacking radios, they used bugles to signal their men to charge. The highlands of North Korea exploded into a nightmare of blaring bugles, shells bursting in the darkness, and masses of rushing soldiers. One marine described the determination of Chinese fighting men conducting human wave attacks: "In the first wave everyone would have a weapon. In the second, third, and fourth waves, half didn't. They'd pick up a weapon from a guy dead on the ground who didn't need it anymore."

The Americans, who weeks earlier felt they were on the threshold of victory, now fell back. At the same time the Korean winter roared out of the north. Temperatures dropped below zero Fahrenheit (17.8 degrees Celsius), and

Marines tough it out in the cold at the Battle of Chosin Reservoir.

17

wind screamed through mountain passes. No troops were in greater peril than the 1st Marine Division trapped at the Chosin Reservoir. Completely surrounded, the marines fought their way through fifty-five miles (88 km) of enemy-held territory to reach the port of Hungnam. "It was impossible to describe the cold," said one marine. "The steel on my rifle was ice. Put bare flesh on it and you stuck, and the only way to get loose was to lose some skin. One time my mouth literally froze shut."

The Marines trapped at the Chosin Reservoir were finally evacuated by ship. For many their suffering did not end with their rescue as hundreds of men had severely frostbitten feet and hands. Doctors treated frostbite victims in various ways, including the amputation of frozen extremities. A sergeant named Sherman Richter explained, "On board ship we were filthy dirty, crummy, had scales on our flesh. They cut our boots off. A doctor walked down the line looking at frostbitten toes [and saying], 'Treatment. Treatment. Amputate. Treatment. Amputate. Treatment. Treatment. . . . ' Everyone held his breath [when the doctor passed him]. If your toes were black, it was too bad for you."

The disastrous turn of events in Korea upset American politics. President Harry Truman fired General MacArthur. Democrats and Republicans quarreled over the war's goals and tactics. Later, as the war dragged on, presidential

TRUMAN VERSUS MACARTHUR

General MacArthur made several public statements that were critical of UN policies governing the conduct of the war. President Truman ordered him to be silent. When MacArthur continued to make such statements, the president fired him. Nevertheless, MacArthur remained a highly regarded figure in the United States, and he was honored with a giant parade in New York City.

President Harry Truman shakes hands with Dwight Eisenhower.

candidate Dwight Eisenhower won votes by promising to visit Korea in hopes of ending the war. Yet no one had an answer as to how to end this dismal struggle.

In early 1951, American-led UN forces halted the enemy advance along a line near the original partition of the 38th parallel. The war slipped into a frustrating **stalemate,** with neither side making dramatic gains in territory. Instead, the

American and North Korean Officers negotiating cease-fire, October 11, 1951.

opposing armies waged costly battles over key hills. Fighting was savage over these hills, most of which had no names. Americans gave these rises and ridges nicknames: "Pork Chop Hill," "Old Baldy," "Bloody Ridge."

A combat engineer named Lenoise Bowman remembered one ferocious battle waged in the middle of the night: "All hell really broke loose. Tracer [bullets] were flying in all directions so thick and fast it was like a storm. . . I felt bullets thudding into my fieldpack, then a sharp pain in my left hand. A bullet had torn my rifle apart. My buddies left and right got hit. Our medic was hit in the top of his head, scattering his brains all over. . . . When I stood up tracers were flying thick all around me. I cannot imagine how I wasn't cut to ribbons."

Armistice talks between the UN and the Communists started in July of 1951, but the negotiations did not halt the fighting. At some stages, U.S. casualties (killed and seriously wounded) totaled 2,500 a month. Gloom settled over the American front. Troop morale sank. Everyone asked the same question: "When are we going home?"

Americans at home **coped** with the frustrations of Korea by trying to ignore the conflict. That was not difficult to do since this struggle lacked the passion and sense of mission that civilians felt as they worked for victory in World War II. The Korean War had no terrible trigger, such as the 1941 Japanese attack on Pearl Harbor that sent a **vengeful** nation storming into action. A general feeling of war weariness also gripped the nation. Only five years had elapsed since the end of World War II, and the public naturally wanted to push this new war out of its thoughts. News from the **static** battlefront slipped from the first page in the papers to the second or third page. Soon readers had to skip to pages five or six to find reports on the war.

But it was impossible for citizens at home to turn their backs completely on the horrors taking place in Korea. In the first twelve months alone, almost seventy thousand

CASUALTY CONFUSION

For many years the total number of U.S. war deaths in Korea was listed at 54,246. This is the number **etched** in stone at the Korean War Veterans Memorial. But in the late 1990s the Defense Department revised this total downward to 36,914. Officials blamed a clerk, who in the 1950s mistakenly included noncombat deaths as part of the total.

Americans were killed or wounded in the fighting. Again and again, families would receive telegrams from Washington informing them that they had lost a son, a brother, or a husband. Those telegrams brought news that shattered families, just as they did in previous wars. Even in a forgotten war the loved ones of fallen soldiers suffer unbearable agony.

Peace talks continued, and finally a cease-fire date was arranged between the American-led UN forces and the Communists. On July 27, 1953, a sudden silence fell over the frontlines, and the Korean War came to an end. The war had lasted just over three years. Some 1.5 million U.S. servicemen and servicewomen served in Korea. More than thirty-six thousand

American and Communist leaders exchange credentials at the opening session of the Military Armistice Commission talks to end the war.

Americans lost their lives. At the end of the war, much of Korea looked like a moonscape, a land horribly scarred by bombs and shells. Counting soldiers and civilians on both sides, an estimated 2.5 million people were killed during the conflict. The war had no winners. The fighting stopped almost where it began, along a line very near the old 38th parallel. Ever since, the two Koreas have remained divided and sometimes hostile countries.

In the 1960s the United States entered the Vietnam War, initiating yet another clash between Communist and anti-Communist forces. Vietnam was fought because of the same "domino theory" that had ruled military thinking during the

A student anti-Vietnam rally, 1968

Korean conflict. The domino theory held that if one country fell to the Communists, then its neighbors—like a line of dominos tipping into each other—would also fall. From its beginnings, the Vietnam War was unpopular because many Americans saw it as unjust. The 1960s, unlike the silent 1950s, was an **activist era.** Beginning in 1965 and extending to 1973, college students and peace **advocates** rallied repeatedly on city streets to demand that their political leaders pull America's troops out of Vietnam. Other than the Civil War (1861–1865), the Vietnam War divided the nation more than any armed struggle in its history.

American forces withdrew from Vietnam in 1973, marking the first time the United States had ever lost a war. Even though the war ended, memories of it continued to trouble the country. In an effort to finally heal the wounds of the conflict, the Vietnam Veterans Memorial was built along the National Mall in Washington, D.C. Its dominant feature is two black granite walls on which the names of the more than 58,000 Americans killed in Vietnam are engraved. The monument did, indeed, help heal the nation's wounds, and for this reason it is sometimes called "The Wall of Healing." Shortly after it was erected, the Vietnam Veterans Memorial became the most visited shrine in the nation's capital.

PRESIDENTIAL WARS

The Constitution gives Congress the sole power to declare war, but it also says, "The president shall be commander in chief of the Army and Navy." The role of commander in chief gives the president the power to conduct military actions. Both the Korean and the Vietnam wars were fought by order of the president, without an official declaration of war passed by Congress.

A seven-year-old girl touches the names on the wall at the Vietnam Veterans Memorial.

25

BIRTH OF A MONUMENT

The Vietnam Veterans Memorial prompted a burning question: Why was there no such monument for the forgotten veterans of the Korean War? That question was asked by, among others, Hal Barker, whose father had served as a helicopter rescue pilot in Korea.

Young Hal Barker grew up hearing a story about one of his father's wartime experiences. Near a savagely fought-over hill called Heartbreak Ridge, Barker's father attempted to pick up a fighter pilot whose plane was shot

Hal Barker, left, and his brother Ted Barker, photographed with their Korean War Project Web site displayed

✳ ✳ ✳ ✳

down behind enemy lines. Again and again his father tried to make the rescue, but each time his helicopter was driven off by rifle and machine-gun fire from the ground. The downed pilot was later reported as missing in action and presumed dead. The rescue attempt won Barker's father a Silver Star for gallantry, but he refused to talk about the incident. "I couldn't get him" was all he would say.

After researching the mission, Hal Barker discovered the fighter pilot was a young man from Chicago named Art DeLacy. Barker contacted DeLacy's family in Chicago, and they became friends. DeLacy was a forgotten casualty of the Korean War, and Barker's father was a forgotten hero of the conflict. Why should this be? When would the nation recognize those who served in the Forgotten War?

In December 1984, Hal Barker helped to establish the Korean War Memorial Trust Fund. Its purpose was to raise money to build a monument honoring those who fought in the Forgotten War. Barker donated the first $10 raised for the fund in the memory of fighter pilot Art DeLacy. Eventually, $17 million was raised. The total cost to build the monument was $18.1 million. No tax money was used to build the monument. Funds were collected entirely through private donations. Remarkably, about $13 million of the total raised was given in small contributions from Korean War veterans. Another $2.5 million came from large South Korean firms such as Hyundai and Samsung. Various individuals and organizations contributed the remaining money.

In October 1986, President Ronald Reagan signed the Korean War Veterans Memorial Act, which gave government support to the project. Early on, it was determined that the monument would be built along the National Mall, near the famous Reflecting Pool and the **brooding** statue of Abraham Lincoln. It was also decided that the memorial should be a national memorial. A memorial is

U.S. President Bill Clinton and South Korean President Kim Young Sam at the dedication ceremony.

A view down the National
Mall in Washington, D.C.

THE NATIONAL MALL

The National Mall is the inspirational heart of

Washington, D.C. A two-mile (3.2 km) walkway of

grass and shade trees, the mall stretches from the

U.S. Capitol building to the Lincoln Memorial. Most

of the 20 million tourists who come to the capital

each year visit the mall.

an object, often a statue, that tells the story of a person or event. A national memorial stands as a symbol of importance to all Americans. The Vietnam Veterans Memorial is a national memorial that reminds its visitors of the sacrifices made by Vietnam veterans. The huge statue nearby, the Lincoln National Memorial, honors the memory of the beloved sixteenth president.

REALIZING THE DREAM

What sort of shrine should be raised to remind Americans of the Forgotten War? More than five hundred artists submitted designs for the memorial. New memorials in Washington always provoke arguments among artists, city planners, and architects, and this was no exception. The experts clashed over where to place the new monument and how it should look. Such disagreement delayed construction of the World War II Memorial until the year 2001, more than fifty-five years after that war concluded. Planning for the proposed Korean War Veterans Memorial brought up many questions. For example, would the monument be too militaristic?

Frank C. Gaylord II, right, sculptor of the statues for the Korean War Veterans Memorial

Would it represent all Americans who served in Korea? In the end it took more than nine years to design and build the memorial, three times longer than it took to fight the war.

A Washington architectural firm called Cooper Lecky was named as the general contractor. Earlier, that same firm had built the Vietnam Veterans Memorial. Frank C. Gaylord II was chosen as the principal sculptor. Gaylord set to work creating the statues of infantrymen marching in a triangular formation called the "Field of Service." The individual statues that were built were just over seven feet (2.1 m) in height—tall but not overly imposing. Some suggested that the figures should be charging, with fixed bayonets and battle cries on their lips. Gaylord rejected this notion. As a World War II combat veteran, he had experienced the horrors of war, and did not want to glamorize warfare. "Their idea of combat was John Wayne [movies]," said Gaylord. "I can tell you the truth, the thing I needed most my first day in combat was my mother."

The patrol of nineteen gray steel statues in the Field of Service is the first part of the monument you see when you approach it. Look closer and you will notice that the men on this patrol are wearing the uniforms of the U.S. Army, Navy, Air Force, and Marines. They also represent a variety of ethnic groups. All are covered with windblown ponchos as protection against the hostile Korean weather. Many Korean War veterans claim that the Field of Service is best experienced during winter's sleet and snow. Visitors may read

THE IMMORTAL NINETEEN

At first thirty-eight statues of servicemen were proposed for the monument, representing the 38th parallel. But thirty-eight figures were thought to be too many for the limited space, and so the number was cut to nineteen.

The Field of Service, photographed in the snow

33

SOLID STATUES

The steel statues in the Field of Service were built to last; they weigh about 1,000 pounds (450 kg) each.

what they wish on the faces of the men—fear, courage, determination, homesickness, sadness, pain. "It looks just like us when we went out on patrol," said a Korean War soldier named Richard Schimmel, from Des Plaines, Illinois. The patrol is marching toward the American flag, a symbol of home. Inscribed below the flag are the words

OUR NATION HONORS
HER SONS AND DAUGHTERS
WHO ANSWERED THE CALL
TO DEFEND A COUNTRY
THEY NEVER KNEW
AND A PEOPLE
THEY NEVER MET

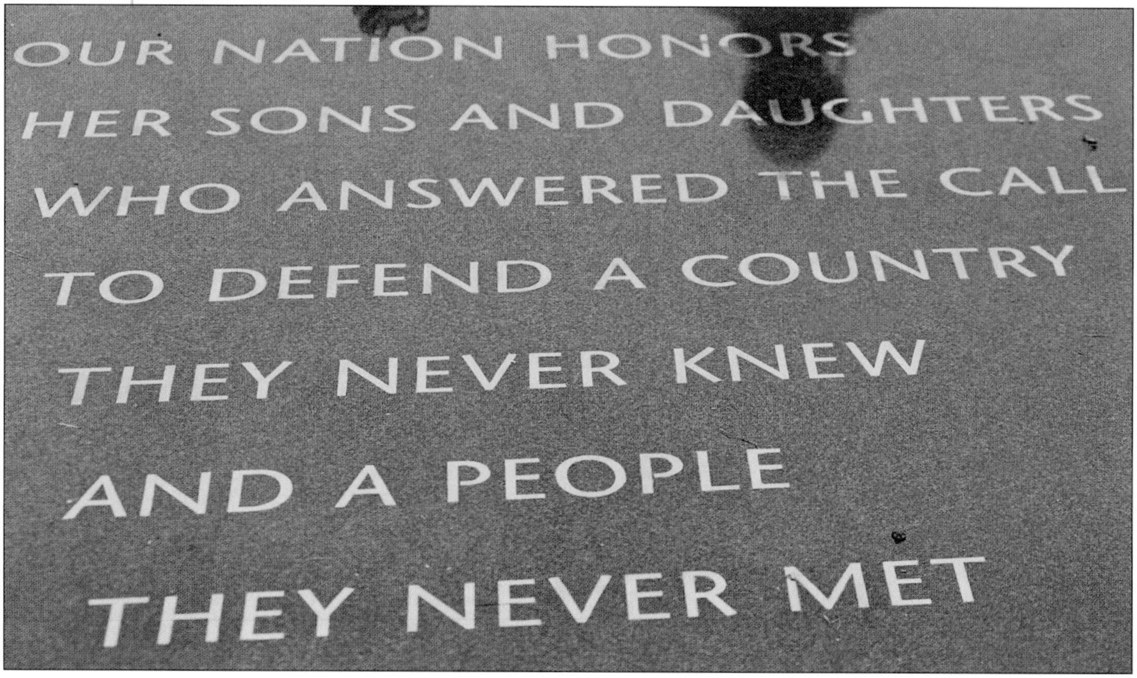

The wall of the Vietnam Veterans Memorial is covered with names of the tens of thousands of Americans killed or missing in action in Vietnam.

North of the Field of Service is a granite block listing the member countries of the United Nations that sent troops to Korea. To the south is the intriguing wall of black granite bearing the simple snapshots of men and women. All soldiers take pictures of themselves and their buddies. Designers of

WALL OF FACES

The wall was designed by Louis Nelson and is 164 feet (50m) long. In addition to the faces of fighting men, it contains pictures of clerks, nurses, doctors, and chaplains.

the memorial combed through the National Archives and selected 2,400 such photos from the Korean War. The images were **etched** onto the granite face of the wall with a computer-guided stencil. As the Vietnam wall contains the names of its heroes, this wall bears the faces of the Korean War heroes. The photo images on the wall are unnamed, and many of those shown did not come home. Sometimes a visitor will jump with joy when he or she sees the image of a father, a brother, or an uncle.

The wall, the Field of Service, and a circular pond called the Pool of Remembrance make up the Korean War Veterans Memorial. Tourists claim that you can go there ten times and see something different in the complex with each visit. Some like to visit the memorial at twilight or at night, when the statues, the wall, and the pool seem to radiate a special spiritual feeling.

A statue at dusk

WELCOME TO THE KOREAN WAR VETERANS MEMORIAL

Admission to the memorial is free. The Korean War Veterans Memorial covers 2.2 acres (0.9 hectares) of ground in the heart of the nation's capital. This, and all other national memorials, are administered by the National Park Service. Uniformed guides, called rangers, are on duty at the memorial every day except December 25. The rangers are happy to answer questions. If you wish to write, address inquiries to:

Superintendent, National Capital Parks—Central
900 Ohio Drive, SW
Washington, DC 20024-2000
Phone: (202)619-7222

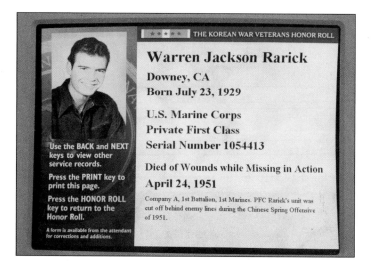

The Korean War is also remembered on the Web at such sites as *http://www.americanwardead.com/search.htm*, shown here.

Rising above the monument are words chiseled into stone: FREEDOM IS NOT FREE. In the minds and hearts of the veterans this message serves as the theme of the Korean War Veterans Memorial. Those veterans fought in an unpopular and misunderstood conflict. War-weary people at home did their best to ignore the fight raging on the other side of the world. The conclusion of the war is seemingly meaningless. In terms of territory won and lost by either side the three-year-long struggle changed nothing. Today many historians think of the Korean War as a disastrous mistake. It is no wonder it became the Forgotten War. But the veterans believe that by going to Korea they did their duty as citizens of a free country. Perhaps the Korean War veterans are the only ones who truly understand the message: FREEDOM IS NOT FREE.

★ ★ ★ ★

As long as the Korean War Veterans Memorial stands, the Korean War will no longer be the Forgotten War. On the day the monument was dedicated, Angus Deming, the lieutenant who led a platoon of marines in 1951, wrote: "[We] answered the call simply because our country needed us. Our only anger, really, was that so much bravery, so much uncomplaining devotion to duty, went unrecognized for so long. Now that lingering bitterness has been laid to rest at last."

Visitors frequently leave gifts like flowers and flags at the Korean War Veterans Memorial.

Glossary

activist era—a time of great activity, usually meaning political activity

advocates—those who promote or favor a certain cause

brooding—a thoughtful, pondering mood

coped—put up with, or survived, a troubling time

etched—to finely write on, or imprint an object

parallel—in geography, an imaginary straight line that serves as a boundary

peninsula—a long, narrow portion of land stretching out into water

poncho—a raincoat with a hood

relentless—a term used to describe a force that does not give up

stalemate—a draw in a contest

static—when referring to action, an adjective describing
an object that does not move

subtly—not obvious, having an almost hidden meaning

vengeful—desiring to get even for an insult or damage

Timeline: Korean War

1910	1945	1945 - 1950	1950	1951	1952	1953

| | | | **JUNE 25** War breaks out in Korea when the North Korean army invades South Korea. | **APRIL 11** President Truman fires General Douglas MacArthur. | Although the fighting is horrific, the battlefronts in Korea are stagnant; gradually the U.S. public loses interest in the war and becomes impatient for an end to hostilities. | After long and frustrating negotiations, a cease-fire is arranged for July 27 and the Korean War comes to an end. |
| Japan occupies the entire Korean Peninsula. | At the close of World War II, Russian forces march into North Korea; the 38th Parallel is created to separate U.S. and Russian occupying armies. | At first all parties believe the 38th Parallel will be temporary, but separate and hostile governments develop in North and South Korea. | **SEPTEMBER 15** U.S. forces land behind enemy lines at Inchon Harbor. **OCTOBER 25** China enters the war on the side of North Korea. | **JULY 10** Truce talks begin between Communist and U.S.-led forces, but the fighting continues. | | |

Memorial

1982
The Vietnam Veterans Memorial is built along the National Mall in Washington, D.C.

1984
The Korean War Memorial Trust Fund is established to raise money to build a monument to Korean veterans.

1986
President Ronald Reagan signs the Korean War Veterans Memorial Act, which gives government support to the project.

1995
The Korean War Veterans Memorial is dedicated on July 27 in a ceremony led by President Bill Clinton.

45

To Find Out More

BOOKS

Choi, Sook N. *Echoes of the White Giraffe*. Boston: Houghton Mifflin, 1993.

Gay, Kathlyn and Martin Gay. *The Korean War*. Brookfield, CT: 21ˢᵗ Century Books, 1996.

January, Brendan. *The National Mall*. Danbury, CT: Children's Press, 2000.

Smith, Carter. *The Korean War*. Parsippany, NJ: Silver Burdett, 1996.

Stein, R. Conrad. *The Korean War: The Forgotten War*. Berkeley Heights, NJ: Enslow Publishers, 1994.

Steins, Richard. *The Post War Years: The Cold War and the Atomic Age (1950–1959)*. Brookfield, CT: 21ˢᵗ Century Books, 1994.

ONLINE SITES

National Park Service/Korean War Veterans Memorial
http://www.nps.gov/kwvm

Korean War Project
www.koreanwar.org

Index

Bold numbers indicate illustrations.

About the Author

R. Conrad Stein was born in and grew up in Chicago. At age eighteen he joined the United States Marine Corps and served three years. After his discharge he attended the University of Illinois and graduated with a degree in history. Mr. Stein is a full-time writer. Over the years he has published more than one hundred books for young readers. The author lives in Chicago with his wife (children's book author Deborah Kent) and their daughter, Janna.

Mr. Stein enlisted in the marines in 1955, two years after the conclusion of the Korean War. Many of his marine friends were Korean War veterans who had survived terrible fighting during that conflict. The author has visited the Korean War Veterans Memorial many times. He believes it is a stunning monument, and he is delighted that the nation has finally honored the men and women who served in the Forgotten War.